GAUCHADA

BY C. Drew Lamm

ILLUSTRATED BY Fabian Negrin

ALFRED A. KNOPF

New York

To Linda, who crossed the ocean wearing the moon before me

Constance, who's sharp and alive
Kate, who has always been true
Molly, who listens to leaves
Ellery, who smiles when she dreams

And Nancy, who chose this story to give to you . . .
—C.D.L.

To the thirty thousands who flew away
—F.N.

THIS IS A BORZOI BOOK PUBLISHED BY ALFRED A. KNOPF
Text copyright © 2002 by C. Drew Lamm
Illustrations copyright © 2002 by Fabian Negrin
All rights reserved under International and Pan-American Copyright
Conventions. Published in the United States of America by
Alfred A. Knopf, a division of Random House, Inc., New York,
and simultaneously in Canada by Random House of Canada Limited,
Toronto. Distributed by Random House, Inc., New York.

KNOPF, BORZOI BOOKS, and the colophon are registered trademarks
of Random House, Inc.

www.randomhouse.com/kids

Library of Congress Cataloging-in-Publication Data
Lamm, C. Drew.
Gauchada / by C. Drew Lamm ; illustrated by Fabian Negrin.
p. cm.
Summary: A necklace is lovingly passed from one person to another,
traveling much farther than the Argentine gaucho who made it will
ever go.
ISBN 0-375-81267-9 (trade) — ISBN 0-375-91267-3 (lib. bdg.)
[1. Necklaces—Fiction. 2. Argentina—Fiction.] I. Negrin, Fabian, ill.
II. Title.
PZ7.L1817 Gau 2002
[E]—dc21 00-067795

Printed in the United States of America
February 2002
10 9 8 7 6 5 4 3 2 1
First Edition

In Argentina there is an expression, "to make a *gauchada*." It means to do something kind, something with love, without expecting anything in return.

Some other words in this story that may be unfamiliar:

A *gaucho* is a cowboy. The *pampas* are flat, fertile plains. The grasses of the pampas stretch across the land like an ocean. Just sky and grass except for an occasional gnarled *ombu* tree, a vital source of shade. This is where the gauchos roamed before the pampas were divided and fenced. *Maté* is a strong Argentine tea. A gourd filled with this tea is often passed from hand to hand and sipped from a communal silver straw, the *bombilla*. It is said that a foreigner who drinks of the maté will always long to return to Argentina. A *quebrada* is a wide valley, the perfect place to herd cows. And a *zamba* is a lively dance originated by the gauchos.

In an open space where cows graze,
   a gaucho, an Argentine man, sits carving.
      He works with hands, dirt-lined and leathery,
         carving a piece of old bone into a crescent moon.
            There's music in his hands and he sings as he carves.

He pauses to sip maté, his gaucho tea, through his worn bombilla.
Then he chooses silver. Silver to frame the moon.
Silver to shine on the edge of the bone.
    He places a black stone beside the moon
    and attaches a fine chain.
    "Esta completo."
            You would buy this necklace if you could,
            but money slides off its silver chain like rain off the pampas grass.
                    This moon will be given.

Perhaps after the rains have again greened the pampas,
perhaps after the cows stampede through the quebradas,
perhaps after he has danced a thousand zambas,
sometime after that . . .

the gaucho who chose the bone
and smoothed the silver
and placed the stone
will know.

As he knows before thunder's roar of the rain that will pour,
   as he knows before the cow lies down that the calf will be born,
     just as he knew this chip of bone would be moon . . .
      the gaucho will know where the necklace will go.

First to a grandmother sharp and alive behind old eyes.
He places the moon around her soft neck.

One day deep in her soul, she knows to whom the gift of the moon bone goes.
To a mother listening to leaves of a lone ombu tree
as they touch in the breeze.
She feels silver beneath her chin, until one day . . .

. . . a girl who smiles when she dreams feels the cool of the moon in her palm.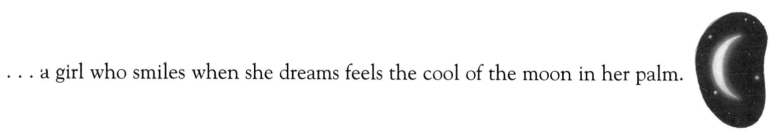

The moon and the stone travel farther than the gaucho will ever roam.

It lives a thousand lives.

It crosses the ocean.
The moon rises and falls
as a writer spins
with pencils and whims.

And like the women before her, someday she will know.
As she knows before winter that the pond will freeze,
   as she knows before the downbeat her heart will lead,
      just as she knows before words the story she'll weave,
         she will know where the gift of the moon will go.

Perhaps to a baby who's shimmering new,
   perhaps to a friend who has always been true . . .

. . . perhaps to you.

And you will tell of an open space
    where cows stamp the land and champ the pampas . . .

. . . and a gaucho, an Argentine man, sits carving.